AF489799

Your Arrival

Put your picture when you were a baby here

Full name: _______________________

Date of birth: _______________________

Place of birth: _______________________

Were you born in a hospital? if not, where?

Was there anything unusual about your birth?

Were you named after a relative or someone else of significance

What have your parents told you about how you were as a baby?

What were your first words?

Are there any stories about when you were a baby

Your
Roots

Family Tree

Family Tree

My Great Grandfather

My Great Grandfather

My Great Grandmother

My Great Grandmother

My Grandfather

My Grandfather

My Grandmother

My Grandmother

My Mother

Every Picture Has a Story

Your Family

Every Picture Has a Story

Describe your parents when you think of them, which of their characteristics stand out the most?

How did your parents meet? what do you think they liked most about each other?

How did your parents enjoy spending time together?

Write about your memory of a pleasant time with one or both of your parents.

What is the most embarrassing thing your mother or father ever did to you?

What did your parents do to earn a living? Did they like their jobs?

What were your parents' favorite hobbies? Did they had any special talents?

How did you spent time with your parents?

What were the most important things you learned from your parents?

What stories did your parents tell you?

How are you and your parents alike and different?

What do you admire about each parent?

Write a summary of your parents' life thus far.

How many siblings do you have and where do you fall in your family?

Describe your siblings when you think of them, which of their characteristics stand out the most?

Did you know your grandparents very well? What do you
remember most about them?

____

____

____

____

____

Where did your grandparents on both sides come from?

____

____

____

____

____

What did you call your grandparents? where did these
nicknames come from?

____

____

____

____

____

How did you spent time with your grandparents?

____

____

____

____

____

____

____

____

What are your favorite stories that grandpa/grandma told you?

____

____

____

____

____

____

____

____

____

What were the most important things you learned from your
grandparents?

Are there any other family members you particularly remember?
What makes them stand out in your mind?

Record the history of items you consider to be family heirlooms.
The heirloom doesn't have to be valuable, so long as it is important to the family.

Write about a birth in your family that changed everything

Write about a death in the family that changed everything

How do you celebrate birthdays in your family? Write about your feelings about past birthdays.

Write about your family stories of sacrifice?

What's your role in your family?

How do you define 'family'?

Growing Up

Every Picture Has a Story

What is your earliest childhood memory?

If you could go back to one day in your childhood, which day would that be? Why?

Who was your best childhood friend? Write about some of the fun things you used to do together.

Can you remember your mom's or grandmother's kitchen? Use sight and smell words to describe it.

Did you have any nicknames? How did you get them?

How did you celebrate the holidays?

What was your favorite hobby?

What was the best and worst part of your childhood?

Where did you grow up when you were a kid?

What were your favorite childhood shows and characters?

What were the things do you were doing for fun in your childhood?

What was the worst trouble you remember getting into as a kid?

How did you pull yourself out of ruts during tough times in your childhood?

How did you handle peer pressure when you were a kid?

Write about some sayings, expressions, or advice you heard at home when you were growing up. Who said them? What did they mean? Do you use any of those expressions today?

When you were a child, how did you imagine your adult self?

Do you have any favorite stories from your childhood?

Education

Every Picture Has a Story

What are the names of schools and dates you attended Primary
School, high school, colleges, trade or technical schools?

What are your earliest school day memories?

Talk about how you got to school each day? Think back to the details
of this, record your memories of the sights, sounds, feelings of that.

What did you learn in those first years of school that you would like to pass along to the next generation

Were you involved in sports, music, drama, or other extracurricular activities

Write about a person from your school who has really made a difference in your life.

How did you get through hard times with bullies at school?

Describe your feelings at the start of the school year. Did you regret the ending of summer freedoms or look forward to school?

What kind of grades did you get in school?

What are your best memories of grade school/high school /college/graduate school? Worst memories?

Do you have any favorite stories from school?

Teenage Years

Every Picture Has a Story

Put a picture about this chapter here

How did you get through hard times in your teenage?

What do you know now that you wish you'd known when you were a teenager?

What were the hot fashion trends in your teens?

How did you dress and style your hair during your teens?

What were the things do you were doing for fun in your teenage?

What have you learned in your teens?

Who was your best teenage friend? Write about some of the fun things you used to do together.

Did you date in high school? Did you have any girlfriends in your teen years?

What did a typical Friday night look like for you at your teenage?

Knowing all you know now, what advice would you give your teenage self?

What was the best and worst part of your teens?

Do you have any favorite stories from your teenage?

Love
and
Relationships

Every Picture Has a Story

How did you meet mom? How was your first date?

What are some of your early and best memories together?

What do you remember most about your wedding day?

Did you have a honeymoon? Where did you go?

What were the challenges in your relationship?

What are some of your best fun memories together?

How do you keep your relationship strong?

Do you believe in love at first sight?

Thinking of your relationship, what advice would you give a young person, such as your children?

Discuss the idea of romance. Does it work in real life? Do you believe in it?

How do you tell if you are really in love? Write about what true love means to you.

How many serious relationships were you in before you settled down (if you did)? What were they like?

What are your beliefs about marriage?

What are the most meaningful relationships in your life?

How should you handle the end of a friendship?

Write about the first person who broke your heart. Write about them in first person present tense.

Do you have a story about a friend who broke your trust? Write about how it made you feel when it happened and how you feel about it today.

Becoming A Parent

Every Picture Has a Story

Talk about what was going through your head when you first got to know that you become a parent?

Tell me about when you found out you were going to have me.

Tell me the story about my birth.

How did you feel about raising your children? What was the best part? The hardest part?

What was the hardest part about me growing up?

What was your biggest fear about raising kids?

Did you ever want more children?

What kind of parent did you think you would be? And what kind of parent do you think you ended up being?

What's your favorite thing about being a parent?

Did your views on religion/sex/family dynamics/politics
change because of having kids?

Do you think I will be a good parent?

Adulthood

Every Picture Has a Story

What was the happiest time in your adult life so far? Why?

What was the hardest time? How did you get through it?

What were the most important values you wanted to teach your family?

Did you and your friends have a special place to hangout?

What was your first car? What did you pay for it? How did you pay for it?

Who are your closest friends to this day? Who is your oldest friend?

What were the hardest choices you ever had to make?

Was there a person or event that really changed the course of your life?

What was the scariest thing that ever happened to you?

What activities have you really enjoyed as an adult?

What are your hobbies?

What is your passion and how did you get started with it?

What have you done to earn money?

What was your first job and how did it go?

Write about how you felt the first time you were fired from a job or had to quit.

What are you proudest of in your career?

What are some amazing things that have happened to you?

Do you have any favorite stories from your Adulthood?

Your Personality

Every Picture Has a Story

What is your personal credo?

What motivates you?

What makes you happy?

What are you good at?

How much self-control do you have?

How good are you at waiting for what you really want?

If you feel sad, what do you usually do to make yourself feel better? Do you prefer to be on your own or with somebody?

How stressed are you? How do you relieve stress?

How well do you perform under pressure?

How well do you take criticism?

Are you hard or easy on yourself?

Do you have a hard time making decisions?

How good are you at time management?

How productive and organized are you?

How competitive are you?

Do you perform better when you're competing or when you're collaborating?

How do you react when provoked?

How often do you cry?

Do you think you're brave?

What are your fears and phobias?

Do you like being alone?

Are you more introvert or extrovert?

Are you a nerd or a geek?

Talk more about your personality

More About You

Every Picture Has a Story

What is something I still don't know about you?

Your best qualities are

Your worst qualities are

Have you ever been addicted to something or someone?
Are you still struggling with this?

What's the best trip you've ever taken?

Do you like to exercise? How has exercise changed your health, your body or your life?

What are you most grateful for?

What do you think about religion?

Tell a story about a lie you told that everybody still believes. Why did you lie and why haven't you told the truth?

Don't judge a book by its cover. But we do, don't we? How do you judge people based on their appearance?

What's the best gift you've ever received?

What's the highest honor or award you've ever received?

What's the most memorable phone call you've ever received?

What are the best compliments you ever received?

What's the one thing you've always wanted but still don't have?

Is there anything you always wanted to tell me but never have?

Who is your role model? Who are your heroes?

What or who is your favorite:

Animal?

Artist?

Athlete?

Author?

Board game?

Book?

Candy?

Card game?

Color?

Cookie?

Drink?

Flavor of ice cream?

Flower?

Holiday?

Meal?

Movie star?

Movie?

Musical group?

Musical instrument?

Painting?

Restaurant?

Season?

Singer?

Songs?

Sport?

Reflections & Words Of Wisdom

Every Picture Has a Story

Recall for me five of the most important lessons you have learned in life.

What have you learned over your lifetime that you'd like to share with the younger generation?

Write a story about a time when you refused to give up.

Write a list of "firsts" (i.e. first time you drove a car, first employment, etc.) Select a few and write about how you felt about what happened.

Write about the things that you enjoy most and are most passionate about. Do you feel that you devote enough time to each?

What's the best advice you've gotten?

What are some of the memories you associate with springtime?
With summer, fall, and winter?

Make a list of 10 books you would like your children to read.
Give a reason for each one.

How would you want your loved ones to remember you?

Write about winning something

Write about losing something

What mistakes taught you the most about life?

How do you define a "good life" or a "successful life"?

What do you see as your place or purpose in life? How did you come to that conclusion?

If you were to give advice to me or my children, or even children to come in our family, what would it be?

Do you think about dying? Are you scared?

How do you imagine your death?

Are you where you thought you'd be at this point in your life?

Do you regret anything?

Write about five objects that tell the story of your life?

Creative Space